ISBN 978-0-484-59491-2
PIBN 10051767

This book is a reproduction of an important historical work. Forgotten Books uses
state-of-the-art technology to digitally reconstruct the work, preserving the original format
whilst repairing imperfections present in the aged copy. In rare cases, an imperfection in
the original, such as a blemish or missing page, may be replicated in our edition. We do,
however, repair the vast majority of imperfections successfully; any imperfections that
remain are intentionally left to preserve the state of such historical works.

The Society of Medical Jurisprudence

Proceedings of the 320th regular meeting, held at the New York Academy of Medicine, November 14, 1921.

The minutes of the 319th regular meeting were read and approved; an abstract of the 362nd regular meeting of the Board of Trustees was read for information.

Election to Honorary Membership:

Major-General Leonard Wood.

Election to Memership:

Samuel Wolbarst, Esq., 277 Broadway, N. Y. City.
Stephen Perham Jewett, M.D., 1200 Madison Ave., N. Y. City.
Harry N. French, Esq., 31 Nassau Street, N. Y. City.
Ernest M. Vaughan, M.D., 102 Fenimore Street, Brooklyn.
Samuel Parnass, M.D., 1218 Herkimer Street, Brooklyn.

Nomination of Officers:

For President: Charles Oakes, Esq.*
    John Kirtland Clark, Esq.
For Vice-President: Thomas C. Chalmers, M.D.
For Treasurer: Charles P. Blaney, Esq.*
    John MacKinlay Wight, Esq.
For Corresponding Secretary: Edward E. Hicks, M.D.
For Recording Secretary: L. Howard Moss, M.D.

* Withdrew.

3

Trustees

Scientific Session:

I. Paper: "The Employment of Intelligence Tests in the Control of Immigration."

By G. Alfred Lawrence, M.D.

II. Discussion by Phyllis Blanchard, Ph.D., Smith Ely Jelliffe, M.D., J. J. Stenquist, Esq., Antonio Stella, M. D., Dr. Lazarus.

* Withdrew.

[Reprint from THE MEDICAL TIMES, March, 1922.]

THE EMPLOYMENT OF INTELLIGENCE TESTS IN THE CONTROL OF IMMIGRATION.*

G. Alfred Lawrence, LL.B., Ph.D., M.D.,

Major, Medical Reserve Corps, U. S. A.; formerly adjunct Professor Nervous and Mental Diseases, New York Post-Graduate Medical School and Hospital, New York.

. In the presentation of this subject I wish to first make mention of various factors pertaining to the admission of aliens or foreigners into the United States; secondly, some mention of the extent of crime, insanity, mental deficiency, educational retardation, vocational inefficiency, hereditary abnormality and economic dependency in our midst and the large part the foreign-born element in our Nation play in this difficult problem; thirdly, the rapidly increasing extent to which intelligence tests are being employed to assist in solving such problems; and finally, the applicability of, and the employment of suitably selected intelligence tests in a proper manner by well-qualified and experienced pschiatrists and psychologists as a prophylactic measure and as an aid in the solution of our immigration problem, by excluding a still higher percentage of undesirable aliens than by present methods alone.

It is of vital importance to admit only those of sufficient intelligence, who, at their vocational level, can become good citizens and carry on successfully in their new environment and thus become an economic asset and not a liability or expense to the community at large.

The maudling sentiment that America should receive with open arms the poor and oppressed of all the other nations of the earth, regardless of their mental or physical qualifications should give way to the more sane and human view that only normal units, both physically and mentally, can make for a normal healthy efficient body politics or virile nation, and only such should be allowed to become prospective candidates for citizenship of our great Commonwealth.

According to the latest issued annual report of the Commissioner General of Immigration to the Secretary of Labor, 33,880,104 immigrants passed through regu-

*Read before the Society of Medical Jurisprudence, at the New York Academy of Medicine, November 14th, 1921.

lar channels of our Bureau of Immigration from the year 1776 to 1820 inclusive. Millions of them and their descendants make up a large per cent of the population of the United States today. During the year 1920, 430,-001 entered the United States for permanent residence.

In addition to the above, 191,595 non-immigrant aliens entered the United States for temporary stay—on business, travel, etc. Furthermore, 933,081 alien seamen came into various ports during the same period—making a grand total of 1,566,452 aliens of the above classes entering into the United States for permanent or temporary residence. The largest incidence of permanent immigration to our shores occurred during the year 1907 when 1,285,349 aliens entered the United States for permanent residence in addition to those of the non-immigrant and sailor alien classes, 11,795 of those seeking admission to our country during 1920 were debarred for various reasons—5,297 on the ground that they were likely to become a public charge, 1,639 under the illitcracy test, 1,241 stowaways, 1,164 contract laborers, 541 due to loathsome or contagious diseases, 355 criminals, 353 physical defectives, who, owing to such disability were unable to make a living; 216 insane and other mental defects, 185 prostitutes or guilty of other immoral practices, 291 children under 16 years of age unaccompanied by parents, 60 Chinese, 56 Japanese and 27 natives of other barred Asiatic zones. Of the 216 mental cases, 9 were idiots, 20 imbeciles, 49 feeble minded, 83 insane and epileptic and 38 constitutional psychopathic inferior. There were 61 cases of tuberculosis, 8 chronic alcoholics and 1 alien enemy refused admission.

Two thousand seven hundred and sixty-two aliens were deported after admission, including some 1,500 from insane institutions in all parts of the United States, leaving some 1,500 additional insane in these institutions to be deported at a later date. Russians, however, cannot be deported at present. In addition to the 1,500 insane patients, there were also deported after entry 148 sexually immoral, 292 anarchists, 155 criminals. In these three latter classes, deportation can be effected without regard to length of residence, whereas in the case of aliens who fall into distress here or need public aid from causes arising subsequent to their arrival, they may be deported at Government expense only up to 3 years after landing. It is needless to say that this latter procedure, even if effected, involves a considerable force of assistants and much expense, as these individuals are scattered all over the United States.

The illiteracy test—ability to either read or write some language—went into effect in May, 1917, and since then 5,083 aliens have been excluded and 704 expelled after entry. During 1920, however, 15,094 aliens unable to read or write were admitted under various exceptions to this literacy test—mostly in order to join relatives already in this country. It was estimated that 1,617,018 aliens were admitted into the United States during the period from 1908 to 1918 that would have been excluded had these tests been in effect during that period.

There are some 15 principal ports of entry by which the major portion of aliens enter the United States, including New York, Boston, Philadelphia, Baltimore, Norfolk, Jacksonville, New Orleans, Galveston, San Francisco and Seattle.

At Ellis Island in the harbor of New York the major portion of all aliens enter the United States.

In 1920, 328,269 aliens applied for permanent entry, of which 325,799 were admitted, and 1,722 debarred. Of the latter, 764 were stowaways, 324 illiterate, 264 vagrants, beggars or paupers likely to become a public charge, 170 tubercular or having loathsome or dangerous contagious diseases, 70 were mental defectives including insanity, 86 physically defective, 41 contract laborers, and the balance under miscellaneous statutory charges. About 60 per cent arrive in the steerage and 40 per cent in cabin, and most of the latter enter temporarily.

Each immigrant is examined in line for a fraction of a minute by a medical officer, then sent to the stripping rooms, where partially undressed, he or she receives a rapid general physical examination and if suspected of mental defect is sent to the psychiatrists for further examination. Some 800 or 900 on an average are thus examined daily at Ellis Island at present.

A few months after our entry into the world war, on October 16th, 1918, an Act was passed by Congress empowering the deportations of anarchists, communists and kindred classes and as a result 5,600 warrants were issued and 798 aliens under this class were deported and 591 others await deportation. During the present year,

Congress has further restricted immigration so that at the present time only 3 per cent of the foreign born of any country now represented in the United States can enter in any one year—in other words, if there were 100,000 Spaniards in the United States on January 1, 1921, only 3,000 additional could enter during the following 12 months.

Of the 430,000 immigrants entering the United States in 1920, 106,630 remained in New York, or approximately 25 per cent of the total number.

Past Assistant Surgeon H. Valentine Wildman, Jr., United States Public Health Service, stationed at Ellis Island, N. Y., in a recent article entitled "Mental Examinations of Aliens and their Bearing on the Potential Military Strength of the Nation," among other things states: "Movements of population from one country to another are mainly due to economic causes. They take place usually from the more densely to the less densely populated countries, from those of lower to those of higher standards of life, and from those of lesser to those of greater economic opportunities. It is all the more important therefore that the arriving alien should be physically and mentally fit to compete with others in his new environment and thereby develop a spirit of willingness to render public service in time of need. Public sentiment in the United States appears to favor selection rather than restriction of immigration.

The experience during the war, however, plainly indicates that in the interest of national safety it must be assimilated both in character and numbers. Although physical disability may give rise to dependency, it is only a temporary burden, but insanity and mental defect cause perpetual and increasing burdens to society. Eventually the methods of detecting mental defect should be made so rapid of application that they would be used in all, and in reality be, the measure for admission rather than any literacy requirement." This latter statement is directly in line with our own views, excepting that we believe that the best methods now in vogue, with modifications to apply to the definite problem in hand, should be introduced *at once* as an adjunct to the present methods of examination and as time goes on undoubtedly simple standards of rapid application will gradually be evolved.

For the past 100 years, prior to the world war, 90

per cent of immigration to the United States came from Europe. In 1920, however, only 57 per cent came from that source, the majority of the others coming from Canada and Mexico.

Approximately $3,000,000 was expended by the Bureau of Immigration for the year 1919-1920 and $6,000,-000 was requested for the fiscal year 1920-1921. The officials in charge have repeatedly represented to Congress the totally insufficient appropriation and the inadequacy of the force to properly carry on this tremendously important work for the economic safe guarding of our Nation.

There is now a personnel of approximately 1,700 and there should be at least 2,500. Inspectors begin with a salary of $1,380, and can, after years, reach a maximum of $2,500 a year.

A training school for officers is necessary and would result in greater efficiency and would be of economic value. A proper system of registration of all aliens and a follow-up system at certain intervals for a given period of years after entry would also be of the greatest economic value. At present the Bureau of Immigration is under the Secretary of Labor whereas medical officers of the United States Public Health Service, under the Secretary of the Treasury are intrusted, under the present law, with the physical and mental examination of arriving aliens and seamen. It would seem at first sight to one not versed in all the details and intricacies of this very important work that either one or the other of these Departments or some entirely separate Department should have entire charge and be responsible for the most effective carrying out of the examination and disposition of entering aliens, with a sufficient staff and adequate appropriation.

Of the approximately 110,000,000 population of the United States in 1920 it has been estimated that about 14 per cent are foreign born or to be exact, 13,920,692 are alien born, and a much larger per cent are of foreign born parentage—either one or both parents.

Let us now turn for a moment and see what happens in the course of a year to our population from an economic standpoint: 500,000 of our population died within a period of 5 weeks from influenza during the year 1919-1920; 150,000 died of tuberculosis during this year, 7 to 8 million cases of malaria occurred in the United States during this same period with an economic loss of one billion dollars—over 14 per cent of these at least were foreign born.

During the late world war, 33 per cent of all men presenting themselves for examination at draft boards were physically unfit to fight, due to defects—a large proportion of which were preventable. One of our leading psychologists—an authority upon mental tests—from the examination of the figures resulting from the psychological examination of over 750,000 of the men drafted into our army, has estimated that approximately 50 per cent of the entire population of the United States are of only 12 years, or under, mental age—in other words, have the average mentality of the average 12-year-old child or a lesser degree of mentality.

Some 80,000 of these soldiers inducted into our military force and thus examined were not permitted to go overseas—these intelligence tests indicating that they did not have the intellectual ability to be an effective unit for the work required. This rapid elimination went far in raising the value and effectiveness of those who really did go overseas. Officers and special details for difficult or hazardous service were selected quickly and efficiently by means of these intelligence tests all along the line, and it was almost invariably found that those who performed the best were those who had the highest rating in these intelligence tests.

Seventy-five thousand five hundred and eighty-eight cases of neuro-psychiatry came under observation of the Medical Corps of the United States Army during the world war, or about 2 per cent per thousand of the total military population of the United States, most of whom were eliminated very quickly from active units by means of the intelligence tests and rating.

In addition to their employment in the Army with such valuable results, these intelligence tests have been successfully employed in many other fields of activity with marked economic results—in determining the grade of mentality of the mentally defective, the delinquent, the sexually immoral and perverted the criminal, epileptic, vagrant or dependent, for educational purposes in the determination of the superior, normal or retarded student and for vocational purposes.

In a recent survey, 1920, of delinquency, dependency and feeble mindeness in the state of Oregon for the determination of potential or actual social liabilities conducted by the United States Public Health Service and believed to be the first state-wide cooperative movement in mental and social hygiene by citizens of any State, some 45,000 survey cards were issued and of 3,634 cards returned, 2,502 recorded retardation in school work of one or more years. Over 25 per cent of these showed symptoms of mental defect or dulling, 2,634 of these cases were further analyzed and of the same 234 were recorded as mental defectives, 446 as delinquents and 798 as dependents.

In the winter of 1919-1920 the Utah State Board of Insanity appealed to the Department of Psychology in the University of Utah for aid in conducting a statewide mental survey of the school children of the entire State, excluding Salt Lake City, which maintains its own department of clinical psychology, for the purpose of determining those of superior abilities for educational and vocational purposes, those doing poor or unsatisfactory work because of mental retardation or physical handicap and finally in order to perfect ond standardize a set of group mental tests applicable to the children of Utah, so that the tests could be continued by superintendents and principals of the State after this preliminary survey. A modification of the Army Beta Tests for groups was found best adapted to this purpose. These latter were found to make possible an evaluation of rate of adaptation to a new situation and this is particularly valuable for vocational purposes.

Over 15,000 children were tested and about 5 per cent. found to be in the failing group and it was estimated that 1.11 per cent. of the total school population of Utah were sub-normal. Of the 648 children in the failing group, 44 per cent. were in the first and second grades, 33 per cent. in the third grade, 14 per cent. in the fourth grade and 8 per cent. in the fifth grade—these 5 grades comprising 60 per cent. of the total school population. Undoubtedly some of the 40 per cent. in the higher grades were also subnormal which would increase the percentage of subnormality in the total school population to a slight degree. Many of these children were of foreign born parents, their fathers working in the mines.

Miss Elizabeth J. Farrell, Inspector of Ungraded Classes of the Department of Education of the City of New York, has estimated that there are over 22,200 ungraded children in the public schools of New York City—less than 20 per cent. of whom are now receiving instruction in ungraded classes at an annual expense of approximately $500,000.

These children are mentally retarded and cannot keep up with the regular classes for the average child and will never develop beyond the mental age of 10 years.

In an analysis of 4,771 of these school children in ungraded classes, 500 or 10.48 per cent., were foreign born, 88 per cent. American born and 1.52 per cent. un-ascertained; 3,657 or 70.6 per cent. of these children had foreign born fathers and 3,565, or 74.7 per cent. had foreign born mothers, thus only 19.1 per cent. of these ungraded children had American born fathers and 20.8 per cent. had American born mothers. Most of these foreign born children and parents came from the following countries and in the following numbers:

Nation.	Number of Fathers.	Number of Mothers.	Number of Children.
Italy	1,627	1,584	242
Russia	859	836	143
Germany	264	214	8
Austria	241	244	26
Ireland	221	260	2
Hungary	78	96	9
Poland	69	71	12
England	47	38	13
Roumania	34	26	4
Bohemia	30	29	0
Sweden	25	23	0
Siciliy	23	23	5
France	22	12	3
Scotland	20	17	1
Spain	18	14	4
Greece	12	12	2
Norway	11	10	0
Austro-Hungary	5	6	1

All other countries enumerated had less than 5 of either parent born therein in this series. Of 1,188 other retarded school children intensively studied 70 per cent. were found retarded from one to nine years—44 per cent. will be permanently mentally defective. Only those with an intelligence quotient below 80 were considered mentally abnormal and 2 per cent. of the entire school population is estimated to be mentally defective —mostly morons.

These statistics show the very large percentage of retarded school children in our New York Public Schools who are foreign born or of foreign born parentage, and when we think of the vast sums spent for educational purposes—nearly $44,000,000 in New York City alone, during 1920-1921 it is a matter of serious economic significance. The majority of Italian children are found to be retarded to some degree and their mental level is found to be two or three years below the average native white.

It is found that approximately 40 per cent. of school children fail to progress through the various grades at the expected rate and over $40,000,000 of the $400,-000,000 annually expended in the United States for school instruction is devoted to reteaching children what they have already been taught, but have failed to learn, and this is almost a total loss. The employment of intelligence test primarily would have determined the degree of deficiency, and with the application of even a part of this $40,000,000 for ungraded classes, this economic loss could be entirely avoided and suitable instruction given.

The value and economic importance of the employment of intelligence tests has been recognized at Columbia and other universities. At the 1921 fall examinations of the freshman or entering class at Columbia College all applicants were offered an intelligence examination requiring a total of approximately 3 hours of time and which should be pased satisfactorily by any applicant of normal intelligence who has had a high school training. In many institutions in case of subsequent poor work further intelligence tests are employed and the student directed to take work for which his intellectual ability best fits him, or if unable to select such is eliminated altogether and thus wastes no further time or money in pursuing a course for which he is mentally unsuited. Such intelligence tests are of the greatest value in solving this problem for the student, his family and the educational institution. This brings out the main difference between the usual school examination and an intelligence test—in the former the candidate uses his resourcefulness (and often largely his memory) in solving problems relating to a specific course of instruction, whereas in the latter if properly conducted, he demonstrates his resourcefulness in solving problems which do not relate to any specific school work—he cannot "cram" for this latter examination.

Prior to the development of the intelligence tests the low grade moron was about as high a type of defective as most physicians or even psychologists were able to identify as feeble-minded. By the careful employment of suitable intelligence tests in the hands of experienced psychologists, however, tens of thousands of these high-

grade defectives can be brought under the surveillar
and protection of society, resulting in curtailing the 1
production of feeble-mindedness and the elimination
an enormous amount of crime, pauperism and industr
inefficiency.

Lombroso searched for physical stigmata in crimin;
—the intelligence tests bring out in a definite manr
their mental defects—the real cause of their asocial co
duct—and at least 25 per cent. of criminals are menta.
defective and physical anomalies are simply accompai
ments of feeble-mindeness and their only diagnostic si
nificance is that of indicating mental deficiency. Me
tal weakness and moral abnormality or asocial condt
are closely associated. The value of intelligence tests
dtermining the disposition of cases in our courts
rapidly being recognized and the discriminating jud
in the case of crime, delinquency and all forms of asoc
conduct will refer the case to physicians and psych(
ogists of experience before determining the ultimate d:
position of these cases.

A striking instance of the value of intelligence te;
is shown by the record of 100 girls committed to t
Ohio State Reformitory as with "intellect sound." I
telligence tests given by a competent psychologist r
vealed the fact that 36 per cent. of these girls were u
questionably feeble minded and should of course ha
different care than that of girls of normal intelligen(

Dr. H. H. Goddard, Director of the Bureau of J
venile Research of Ohio, supervised the giving of t
Binet tests in 160 juvenile court cases chosen at rando
in Newark, New Jersey and nearly 50 per cent. we
classified as feeble-minded.

Of 56 delinquent girls from 14 to 20 years of a;
almost 50 per cent. belonged to the 9 or 10 year leve
of 100 prisoners in the Massachusetts State Reform
tory 25 per cent. were feeble-minded. Of 1,186 gii
tested at the State Industrial School at Lancaster, P;
28 per cent. were of subnormal intelligence.

Dr. Katherine B. Davis, former Commissioner (
Charities and Correction of New York City, report(
on 1,000 cases entered at the Bedford Home for W
men in Westchester County, New York and stated th
at least 157 were feeble-minded. Of 564 prostitutes i
vestigated in connection with the Municipal Court (
Chicago, only 3 per cent. had gone beyond the fif
grade in school and it is reasonably certain that 50 p
cent. or more were feeble-minded.

At the Joliet Prison, Ill., 50 per cent. of the female inmates and 26 per cent. of the male inmates were found to be feebleminded. Of 150 delinquents in the Whittier School for Boys at Whittier, Cal., 28 per cent. were feeble-minded and 25 per cent. additional were at or near the border line and in the girls' division the percentage closely agreed with that of the boys.

Of 1,000 young adult prisoners psychologically examined at the State Reformatory, Jeffersonville, Ind., approximately 50 per cent. were found to be feeble-minded.

In his study of cases in the New Jersey State Prisons, Dr. E. A. Doll finds that of the white prisoners some 43 per cent. are foreign born and of these Italians make up 44 per cent. of the foreign born criminals.

The negroes make up about 23 per cent. of the total prisoners. He also finds that the average mental age of the foreign born prisoners is actually below that of the mental average of the negro prisoner and the latter is less than that of the native born white. Furthermore there is a tendency in the foreign born to commit the more serious crimes of murder and assault, whereas, the native white prisoners' tendency is more towards crimes against property than against persons, which requires a higher degree of intelligence to plan and execute.

Of 42 delinquents examined at the New York State Agricultural and Industrial School, at Industry, N. Y., only 6 had American fathers and 7 American mothers, the parentage of 6 fathers and 8 mothers was unknown and the balance were foreign born. Of these children of foreign born parents only 6 had an intelligence quotient of 100.

Dr. Robert H. Gault, Professor of Psychology, Northwestern University and Managing Editor of the *Journal of Criminal Law and Criminology*, kindly forwarded to me the Second Annual Report of the Chicago Crime Commission and on page 34 of this Report the following statement appears: "The problem of immigration, although chiefly a national one and under the exclusive control of the Federal authorities, is one effecting all of the larger cities of the country. Some of the results, as shown by analysis of available criminal records by your Committee, would seem to indicate that there is need for more stringent control at Ellis Island, if not for drastic changes in the Immigration Laws. While it is true that many of the best citizens of the United States emigrated from the Old World to this country, and that each year we receive large numbers of men and women who are most excellent material for American citizenship, the fact remains that the United States continues to be a dumping ground for the riff-raff of Europe."

It is estimated that there are over 45,000 mental defectives in New York State alone and there are 33 states, as determined by the draft which exceed New York in the distribution rates of mental defectives. These detectives are simply children who have never grown up intellectually regardless of their chronological age—less than 10 per cent. of them are idiots and only approximately 4,000 are in proper institutions for their care at a cost of about $3,000,000 annually.

All these cases are potential criminals or prostitutes unless placed in a proper environment. If placed in suitable surroundings, however, most of them are capable of earning a living.

In a recent article entitled "Backward and Defective Children," by the late Dr. Pearce Bailey, Chairman of the New York State Commission for Mental Defectives he states: "According to an estimate made by Dr. Wm. C. Sandy, Psychiatrist to the New York State Commission, 31 per cent. of mental defectives in this State (of N. Y.) are foreign born. Of these Italy furnishes more than any other foreign country. It is true that the excess of foreign born defectives is not much in excess of the foreign born population as a whole (census, 1910), but it should be much less. The immigration laws in regard to the admission of mental defectives are carefully drawn. Why are they not strictly enforced at all ports of entry? Special examinations for the purpose of detecting mental defects should be made at al these ports, although even then all foreign born mental defectives cannot be excluded. Some defective young children will always get by. The Terman Psychological Scale provides for the identification of mental defect at the age of 3 years, but it is difficult to be certain before the age of 4 or 5 years. So we need not expect to prevent the entrance into this country of all foreign born mental defectives, but we can exclude more than we do, and when we do we may expect a decrease in pauperism and crime and in State dependents."

This is significant from the pen of Dr. Bailey who, with the rank of Colonel, was in charge of the Psychiatric Section of the United States Army during the world war. Re-examination at the end of 5 years or less, with provision for deportation in case of feeble-mindedness would provide for the ultimate exclusion of doubtful cases who might be overlooked upon entry.

In addition to the problem of the mental defective as a potential criminal and prostitue in an unfavorable environment is the still more serious problem of their indiscriminate propagation, either by marriage with defectives like themselves, or through illicit relations resulting in the propagation of illegitimate children—thus perpetuating their kind through the inexorable laws of heredity.

A striking illustration of this is the case of Martin Kallikak—a young soldier in the Revolutionary War of English descent—who while visiting at a tavern frequented by militia, met a feeble-minded girl and became the father of her illegitimate feeble-minded son. In 1912 there were 480 known direct descendants of this temporary union and it is known that 36 of these were illegitimate, 33 sexually immoral, 24 confirmed alcoholics, 8 kept houses of ill-fame, 143 were definitely known to be feeble-minded and many others were of questionable mentality. In marked contrast to this record is the following: A few years after returning from the war this same Martin Kallikak married a respectable girl of good family and from this union 496 individuals have been traced in direct descent and in this branch of the family there were no illegitimate children, no immoral women and only one man sexually loose, no criminals, no keepers of houses of ill-fame and only two confirmed alcoholics, not a single feeble-minded individual and most of them were either doctors, lawyers, judges, educators, traders or land-holders.

The Hill Folk—a New England family of English and French origin, and of which 709 persons were traced—of the married women, 24 per cent. gave birth to illegitimate children, 10 per cent. of the women were prostitutes, criminal tendencies were found in 24 members, alcoholism was still more common and 48 per cent. were feeble-minded.

During the past 60 years these Hill Folk have cost the State of Massachusetts in charitable relief, care of feeble-minded, epileptic, insane, correction and punishment for crime, prostitution, pauperism, etc., at least $500,000.

Another notorious family is the Nams derived from a roving Dutchman who settled in western Massachusetts, and of whom 784 have been traced including 187 alcoholics, 232 women and 199 men known to be licentious, 48 inmates of prisons and costing over $1,500,000.

The exact percentage of feeble-minded has not yet been determined, but it was unquestionably a leading trait.

In New York State the Juke family has lived in the Lake Region of the central part of the State for over 70 years, the original ancestor having come from Holland. Five hundred and forty descendants have been traced, of which 20 per cent. were born out of wedlock, 37 known to be syphilitic, 53 been in the poorhouse, 76 sentenced to prison, and of 229 women of marriageable age 128 were prostitutes. The economic loss to the State of New York by this Juke family in 70 years is estimated to be more than $1,300,000, to say nothing of the dissemination of disease, crime, vagrancy, sexual immorality and perversion, promiscuous living in squalid quarters, as squatters on property not their own and constantly shifting about.

The family of Sam Sixty, located in the river bottom region of the Ohio River in the State of Ohio was so designated owing to the fact that the majority of its members had an intelligence rating of 60 or less on the basis of the normal of 100. Of 5 generations investigated in 1915 by Mary Stover Kostir, formerly field worker of the Bureau of Juvenile Research of the State of Ohio, 474 descendants were traced from Sam and Jim Sixty who had been committed to the Ohio Penitentiary convicted of the crime of incest upon one of the daughters of the former, and one of these daughters, 14¾ years old, testing only 8 years mentally, was committed to the Girls' Industrial Home. The father, 47 years old, tested only 8 4/5 years mentally, or 60 per cent. Of 261, from which some definite data was obtainable, 60 had court records and 56 had been in public institutions. Of these, 261, 74 were criminalistic, 77 sexually immoral, 55 alcoholic, 23 prostitutes, 4 epileptic, 3 insane, 3 tramps. Of the crimes perpetrated—burglary, larceny, destruction of property, bootlegging, operating houses of ill-fame, riot, perjury, incest, rape, homicide, shooting to kill and attempting to poison are enumerated; 55 are recorded as feeble-minded, only 3 of normal intelligence and 203 mentality undetermined from lack of data. The majority were poor, shiftless, ignorant, alcoholic, sexually perverted individuals, filthy in habits, using vile language, brutal or abusive, wandering about as tramps, vagrants or hoboes, guilty of assault, wilful destruction of property, burglary, stealing, larceny, extortion and committing of felonies. Many were tubercular, syphilitic or insane, unable to support themselves or families, and inmates, of the work house, correctional or charitable institutions or social dependents. It is needless to say that this family was the cause of an enormous amount of trouble, great expense, and a large economic loss to that community.

Such a record of unrestrained propogation of criminals, moral delinquents and social dependents, with the tremendous cost of their care and financial loss from their social conduct and economic unproductiveness should cause us to use every possible safeguard against the admission of defectives from other countries into our midst and if advertantly they should obtain admission, their prompt deportation to the place from whence they came should be carried out.

The trial of those who become criminals cost the State on an average of $1,000 apiece and some of the chronic recidivists have a record of as high as 20 convictions and many average 3 or more.

There is ample authority under the Mental Deficiency Law of 1919 for the commitment of mentally defective delinquents to custodial care and they should not be placed with the non-criminal mental defective. There were 2,000 vacancies in the penal and correctional institutions of the State of New York in 1920 and with only the additional expense of maintenance the State Legislature could provide that these different institutions should fill their vacancies with such irresponsible criminals and keep them there and prevent their propogation and by vocational means make them largely self supporting. It costs approximately $500 annually for the care of each mental defective in the several institutions for that purpose in this State, but by a suitable colony plan for properly selected cases and placing of other selected cases in families where the defective would be properly safeguarded this expense would be greatly decreased.

As an index of the very appreciable percentage of these delinquents who are either foreign born or are of foreign born parentage, Miss Flora M. Purcell, investigator in charge of the Department of Public Welfare Mental Clinics, prepared statistics of the 812 defectives examined at Dr. Menas S. Gregory's Psychiatric Service at Bellevue Hospital in 1920, of which 239 were committed to Randall's Island, 110 to Craig Colony for epileptics, 239 to Letchworth Village, 37 to Newark, 141 to Rome and 46 to Syracuse State School—the four latter institutions being under the charge of the New York State Commission for Mental Defectives. Of these 812 defectives, 50 were foreign born, 512 were American born of foreign parents, and only 274 American born of American parents. Thus only 33.7 per cent of these mental defectives were native born of native born parents and 66.3 per cent were either foreign born or had foreign born parents.

Dr. S. D. Porteus, director of research of the Training School at Vineland, N. J., in a recent communication to me has made the following interesting observations—he states: "To my mind one of the most serious consequences of improperly controlled immigration is the admission of large numbers of psychopathic cases. At one time, because of the restricted opportunities of travel, I believe that it was true to say that immigrants tended to be a selected class, comprising the more adventurous and enterprising of the population. That at least was our experience in Australia where the type of immigrant of 50 years back was of undoubtedly much higher level than those who have entered the country during recent years. At present, immigration is such a comparatively easy matter that the restless maladjusted individual has the chance to transfer his undesirable person to another country. In an analysis of cases which we have made in this institution, I estimate about one-third of our psychopathic cases are of foreign extraction." Dr. Porteus suggests that conditions, educational and otherwise, are much more stimulating in America than in the countries from which many of our immigrants come. He states further, "The Italian child whose mental level is 2 or 3 years below the average native white, is forced through our school grades at the same rate as the average native white and often breaks down mentally as a result, and this difference in intellectual capacity accounts for the very large percentage of Italians found in all classes of defects, delinquencies and dependents. The foreign born Jew, coming from an atmosphere of repression to that of stimulation, also in many instances breaks down mentally under the stress or cannot carry on to the same degree as the average native born American. Of course, the proper place to take action to diminish the inflow of undesirables is at Ellis Island."

We have thus far seen the very large incidence of foreign born among our criminals and delinquents and the appalling statistics of their unrestricted reproduc- tion.

Let us see what our statistics on insanity indicate. In 1910 there were 187,791 inmates in insane hospitals in the United States, of which nearly 30 per cent were foreign born white. In New York State there are over 40,000 insane men, women and children in hospitals, less than 1,000 of which are in private licensed institutions. The balance are a public charge upon the community at an annual cost of approximately $20,000,000, to say nothing of the economic loss from total unproductivity.

Another point of grave concern is that insanity is on the increase and that more and more annually succumb to the stress and demands of our complex present-day so-called civilization. Only 3.4 per cent of these cases are discharged annually as recovered; 12.4 per cent of all New York State expenditures during 1919 was for the care of the insane alone. Of those patients admitted in 1919, 500 had served our country as soldiers during the world war.

The most important aspect of this subject from our standpoint is the fact that the per capita cost of care and maintenance of each case was $304.09 in 1919, the average hospital residence is 10 years and unless an alien developing insanity within 5 years after entry is detected he cannot be deported. This provision should be repealed and the law so enacted that an alien must be deported at any time after admission should he be- come insane.

Of all admissions to our New York State hospitals for the insane during 1919, 48.8 per cent were foreign born, 2 per cent nationality unascertained, and 49.2 per cent native born; 60 per cent of all those admitted had foreign born parents, 11.3 per cent mixed parentage (one native born and one foreign born), only 25 per cent had native born parents, and 3.1 per cent parentage unknown.

From an economic and eugenic standpoint these fig- ures indicate that the majority of our insane are derived from aliens, and that, and this is the most serious aspect of the case, most of the insanity of the United States is propagated through insane alien ancestry. Of all parents who develop insanity and enter insane hospitals, 25 per cent of the men and 6 per cent of the women are cases of general paresis—an entirely preventable form of insanity, as 100 per cent of all cases of paresis are due to syphilis, an infectious disease and this psychosis is a result of the latter disease.

In the case of epilepsy it is estimated that there are over 20,000 epileptics in New York State alone and practically all are more or less inefficient up to complete dependency and many require institutional care. At the Craig Colony for epileptics at Sonyea, New York, supported by and costing the State over half a million dollars annually, there were 1,609 inmates on January 1, 1921—829 males and 780 females. The per capita cost in the care of these epileptics was $377.92 and approximately 10 per cent of those admitted were foreign born and over 50 per cent of the others had foreign born parents.

The New York State Board of Charities, Division of Eugenics and Social Welfare, in 1917 carried on a very exhaustive survey of the extent and cause sof dependency in the 167,331 inhabitants of Oneida County, New York, and found that 6 per cent of this total population was mentally defective, over 12 per cent of persons other than those in alms houses or other institutions became partial or complete dependents and as such received outdoor relief in various forms; 1.2 per cent were unable to make continuous and adequate reactions to the environment in which they found themselves. All those whose quantilative intelligence fell below 11 or 12 years normal mental level at maturity were considered cases of mental defect, as also were cases showing that other form of mental defect described as affective deviation and while so large a degree determines conduct of social or anti-social value; 1.2 per cent of those outside of institutions received public relief and 9.9 per cent of those now outside of institutions had at some time been inmates of institutions and 23 per cent had relatives who had been institution dependents somewhere at some time prior to this survey. In 49.9 per cent of all admissions to insane hospitals, a family history of insanity, nervous diseases, neuropathic or psychopathic traits was obtainable. Of 53 young felons investigated in this survey, 36 per cent were foreign born, and of these foreign born, 33 per cent were Italians.

Of 180 criminals in prison, 95 were native born and 85 foreign born, and of the latter 64 were Italians. Of those committed to the New York House of Refuge at Randall's Island 33 1/3 per cent were foreign born.

The eugenic make-up of all these types show that recessive unit characters dominate and control making for every sort of anti-social, asocial, pathological and dependent symptom behavior and these individuals thus become dependents in every possible phase of social failure and inmates of all types of charitable and correctional institutions. Society must thus work for the elimination of the unfit and rehabilitation of those not too dangerously handicapped and at environmental levels at which they can adjust themselves.

Of the dependents and economic failures—all supported wholly at the expense of the country, approximately 50 per cent were foreign born, and this is one of the up-State counties with a foreign population much less than that of New York County or counties adjacent to the latter.

The entire number of poor persons supported and relieved in the entire State of New York during the year 1916-1917 was 636,565, of which 545,605 were men and 90,860 were women, or 6.5 per cent of a total State population of 9,689,744 at that time.

The above investigation resulted in drawing the following conclusions as to the ultimate causes of dependency—in such individuals there are hereditary recessive characters which become dominant in their biological make-up, influenced by prenatal and postnatal environmental stresses—processes producing various types of organ weakness and developmental defects and which burden the individual and through him the community, making for subnormal citizens unable to achieve their ambitions or even carry on their ordinary life work in an adequate and efficient manner—thus environmental and individualistic factors must be considered in questions of economic liability. The more complex the civilization the greater and ever increasing effort must be exerted on the part of the individual to meet the requirements of the situation in hand and the reaction efforts of the individual as a social unit determines his conduct in the body politic.

The determination to do certain things, which may or

may not be of social value, springs from mental trends linked to many associations, conscious or subconscious, and if the latter the individual may be unaware, and thus not fully responsible to that extent.

This brings us to the "ultimate behavioristic quotient" which is a resultant of the many factors acting in time and augmenting, deflecting or coloring the main trends of the personality, all of which, lead back to the primal instinctive strivings found in every human being. The adequacy or inadequacy with which the personality is enabled to respond to the imperative demands of reality depends upon the factors derived from the heredity and environment of that particular individual.

With a well-balanced biological intercorrelation of all organs and functions we have adequate and wholesome physical and mental reactions with behavior useful to society—in other words a fully normal individual—such ability to react adequately under stimulus depends upon organ integrity—of all organs—thus normal or abnormal behavior is indicative of adequate or inadequate organ reactions. This proper and adequate adjustment of the whole human organism grows more and more difficult with the ever increasing complexities of civilization. Failure to receive adequate satisfaction out of life promotes desires and imperfect compensatory reactions in seeking an outlet for these wish trends, with resulting cases of social inadequacy, psychosis and allied mental states on the one hand and mental defect and delinquency and dependency on the other.

Our fundamental instincts receive their primal direction for good or evil from the presence of or lack of determiners in unit characters from the ancestral germ plasm. We must therefore search out the facts of heredity, constitutional make-up and environmental stress, which will determine the characteristics of their reactions to environment in the terms of behavior. The mentally, defective, psychotic, epileptic, delinquent and dependent instead of being thought of as insane, feeble-minded, sick, pauper or criminal, should be thought of as human beings with an inadequate biological mechanism which is unable to exhibit adequate symptom behavior or conduct under the usual conditions of their environment and thereby draw attention to their need for scientific medical and social help and enlightenment. Let intellectual misfits therefore be measured by intelligence tests and placed in that groove of society where they will "fit" the best, determine their capability and develop their potential capacity to the limit of developmental possibilities. Select a vocation best fitted to their capacity as above determined. This may mean institutional supervision, community life with supervision by social workers or independent economic existence.

The lesson to be derived from these conclusions is that we should recognize the tremendous importance of the careful and accurate examination and diagnosis of all prospective immigrants and only admit those who will undoubtedly become economic units of value to the Nation.

A sound mind in a sound body is axiomatic and we have seen from the many statistics thus far presented that a large proportion of aliens who have succeeded in entering our portals do not possess these qualifications in spite of the care thus far observed in their admittance. Can we further safeguard ourselves and if so, by what additional means?

Properly selected and carefully conducted group intelligence tests by competent and experienced alienists and psychologists will certainly further limit the entrance of defectives, who become such a tremendous economic burden to our already overtaxed and complex social order. Furthermore we must demand a higher standard of admission both mentally and physically.

Dr. David Starr Jordan, Chancellor Emeritus of Leland Stanford, Jr., University, has stated that a good citizen is one who adequately cares for himself and his family in the environment into which he has successfully adjusted and furthermore contributes something additional of constructive value to the common weal. Let us make this the standard of admission for every alien, and if after admission, it is found that he cannot live up to this standard, deport him, no matter how many years have elapsed since his admission.

In order to accomplish this result what can we do in addition to the methods now in effect? Firstly, we can insist on an adequate appropriation and a larger personnel than at present for carrying on the work, so that more rigid and careful examination can be carried out; secondly, we can insist that field and research workers go to all the countries from which aliens come to our shores and make first hand and exhaustive researches as to the conditions there existing and the quality of prospective immigrants seeking admission to our shores, thirdly, experienced investigators should be kept at the points of foreign embarkation and others accompany them across the ocean in order to further study and ·report upon these prospective alien entrants; and finally and of the greatest importance, carefully planned and suitable intelligence tests should be given to every child above 3 years of age and every man and woman of whatever age that succeeds in passing all the other requirements at either the point of embarkation or point of admission to our country, preferably at the former.

Examinations should be repeated after definite intervals should they be indicated, through proper registration.

Would this cost money? Unquestionably a considerable sum, but a mere fraction as compared to the economic saving in money, higher social efficiency, diminished crime, delinquency, physical and mental disease, dependency and, above all, hereditary transmission of mental inferiority.

Intelligence tests so applied could well be considered as an intellectual insurance far more valuable to the community than life, accident, health or fire insurance.

Some may well ask—what is intelligence, of which so many statements have been made up to the present time in this paper and how can we measure it with any degree of accuracy? This is a most pertinent question and should be answered.

Meumann defines intelligence, from the psychological viewpoint, as the power of independent and creative elaboration of new products out of material supplied by memory and the senses, and from a practical point of view involving ability to avoid errors, to surmount difficulties and to adjust to environment.

Stern defines intelligence as general capacity of an individual consciously to adjust his thinking to new requirements—it is general adaptability to new problems and conditions of life.

Ebbinghaus states: "Intellectual ability consists in elaboration of a whole into its worth and meaning by means of many-sided combination, correction and completion of numerous kindred associations—it is a combination activity."

To simplify the definition and reduce it to its lowest terms we might define intelligence as the mental capacity to adjust satisfactorily to the ever-changing environment of the individual at his level—which means to either a greater average or lesser degree than that of the group to which each particular individual belongs as a member of the human family—if to a greater degree that individual is of superior intelligence, if to the average degree the individual is of normal intelligence, and if to a lesser degree that individual is of an inferior intelligence up to complete absence of intelligence or mental vacuity.

Many psychologists have spent years in examining thousands of individuals of all nationalities, of every age, and of every imaginable social condition and occupation and from the enormous mass of data thus obtained it has been found that the average individual at any age is capable of responding to certain carefully selected tests. These tests have been arranged in definite groups for each year, beginning at the age of 3 years and extending up to the average and superior adult. By many thousands of trials it has been found, for instance, that a child of 10 years of age can only answer the questions and solve the problems that the average 8-year-old child can readily solve, that child has a mental age of only 8 years, although its chronological age is 10 years, and as the so-called intelligence quotient, or ratio of mental age to chronological age is based on 100, or normal, this particular child measures 8/10 of normal and has an intelligence quotient of only 80 instead of the 100 it should have if it passed the tests for the average 10-year-old child.

For many years, two French psychologists worked on this problem and published a provisional scale in 1905. This was modified and improved upon and republished as the Simon-Binet Intelligence Scale in 1908 and again, as further modified in 1911. In 1916, the Stanford Revision of the Simon-Binet Scale was presented and with some further modifications is at present in general use. It was found, however, during our late world war that other tests, but along the same lines, were better adapted for the rapid examination of larger or smaller groups, especially of illiterates who required special tests, and as a result, the so-called Army Alpha and Beta Tests were developed and employed for this particular purpose, the Beta Tests for the illiterates. In addition to these tests there are various other special tests, especially adapted for particular conditions as the pantomine, maze, puzzle, mechanical and performance tests.

For vocational work, for instance, many firms employing large numbers have found it of the greatest economic value to have a trained and experienced psychologist or staff of psychologists examine every applicant for a position and as a result of these special intelligence tests the applicant is either rejected as unsuitable material, or if accepted, placed in that position of greatest economic value to the firm. Many of these organizations have formed schools for the rapid training of those who qualify under these tests. Dr. C. S. Yoakum, who with Dr. Yerkes, had charge of the United States Army Intelligence Testing during the world war, and who collaborated with the latter in a book entitled "Army Intelligence Tests," has succeeded in building up a series of tests by means of which men can be selected for insurance work almost without an error. R. H. Macy & Co., in New York City, have a well-equipped psychological testing plant. The Metropolitan Life Insurance Co. employs intelligence tests in the selection of its office force. There are some 58 concerns that are or have used intelligence tests in the selection of their personnel and the number is rapidly increasing.

In some factory and other operations the moron can perform certain parts of the work as well as individuals of higher intelligence and in some of the simpler operations at the factory of the B. F. Goodrich Co., at Akron, Ohio, manufacturers of automobile tires, morons were preferred for certain parts of the work because they were more amenable to discipline and remain better contented with working conditions.

The above facts show again the great economic value of intelligence tests and impress upon us the lesson—do not put a $10,000 man on a $1,000 job, or vice versa—in other words, get the level of intelligence of the individual and put him at construction work on that level of environment.

Intelligence tests can thus be considered as intellectual measuring rods for the determination of the mental capacity and aptitudes of the individual examined, just as the tape measure gives the size and probable capacity of the various parts of the body for physical exertion.

This rule should be applied in the employment of intelligence tests in the case of the alien—if he enters as a laborer give him an intelligence test a little higher than that for a similar laborer now in our country, for it most be borne in mind that the entering alien is greatly handicapped by limited knowledge of our language, customs, laws and methods of doing things; and furthermore, he has hereditary trends and environmental acquirements from the country in which he and his ancestors were born, many of which must be modified.

All varieties of tests for all varieties of conditions should be carefully tried out and any necessary modifications made at any time, should occasion demand, to the end of carrying on the work at the most effective and efficient level.

It should be borne in mind that the employment of intelligence tests as suggested would simply be an adjunct to all the other examinations now conducted. These latter should be made more rigid and carried out much more thoroughly than the present personnel and appropriation will permit. That this adjunct would be of the greatest value I think there can be no doubt. Furthermore, it is entirely practical. With sufficient appropriation, adequate accomodations and a suitable staff of highly trained psychiatrists, psychologists and social workers, invaluable economic results could be obtained and this would be economic national insurance of the highest order.

Dr. C. E. Seashore, Chairman, Division of Anthropology and psychology of the National Research Council, Washington, D. C., in a recent communication addressed to me, made the following statement: "As to the employment of intelligence tests in the control of immigration, I beg to say that I consider this a matter of great moment at the present time. If we can only admit a small number of immigrants, why should we not exercise some judgment in selecting for admission. Enough work in that type of service has been done in psychology now to make it a comparatively easy matter for us to design such procedures should the government be willing to use them. I think, as a physician, you will realize that emotional stability, moral fitness, health and social attitude are as important as intelligence."

I am entirely in accord with Dr. Seashore's views and believe that our tests should be so developed as to determine these latter attributes as well, and that such can be done.

For the work suggested, a director with the necessary number of assistants, a sufficient number of highly educated and trained psychologists to give suitable group tests and occasional individual tests where indicated, social workers to determine hereditary and environmental conditions and a sufficient clerical staff, a record room, special research bureau—these are some of the agencies by which in time and by rigid application the quality of our alien citizenship could be immensely improved at an economic saving of many billions of dollars to our Government.

In this period of world reconstruction, lessened mental and physical resistance, disorder, discontent, increase in insanity, crime, delinquency and dependency—this period above all is the psychological moment in which our Government should act most vigorously and effectively along these lines.

For such intelligence insurance the cost would be a mere bagatelle as compared to the vast saving in the form of higher and better citizenship and in diminished billions of cost for deficiency and dependency and the increased billions added to our assets in higher and better productivity.

In conclusion, I wish to make grateful acknowledgement to Dr. Phyllis Blanchard, Miss Flora M. Purcell, Miss Elizabeth E. Farrell, Dr. Smith Ely Jelliffe, Dr. Menas S. Gregory, Dr. Stephen P. Jewett, Dr. Irwin J. Sands, Dr. W. C. Billings, Dr. H. Valentine Wildman, Jr., Dr. John S. Richards, Dr. H. M. Johnson, Dr. John B. Watson, Dr. Wm. Healy, Dr. Eliot Frost, Dr. Walter Hill Scott, Dr. L. L. Thurstone, Dr. S. D. Porteus, Dr. C. E. Seashore, Dr. Harold C. Bingham, Dr. Robert H. Gault, and Dr. J. L. Stenquist—all well-known specialists and research workers along these lines—for valuable suggestions and data employed in the preparation of this paper.

142 West 86th St.

Discussion.

Phyllis Blanchard, Ph.D., Resident Phychologist, Bellevue Hospital: When we think of the practical side of putting the intelligence test scheme into effect, there are several things that come to mind. I am concerned not only as to the problem of excluding the feeble minded, but as to the probability of many immigrants being sent back who are not actually feeble minded. There are many cases in which, without the aid of thoroughly trained examiners, mistakes are made. We see that every day at Bellevue. We have cases where, because the examiners have not had sufficient experience or training, individuals have been sent to Randalls Island before being sent back to us for observation, and we find them normal; sometime during the period before commitment, they were in a psychotic or emotional state which rendered them temporarily unable to reason intelligently, and they were arbitrarily pronounced feeble minded and committed. I recall two cases recently sent to us, both of whom Ellis Island was trying to deport on the ground of feeble mindedness. One was a woman who was in the post-syphilitic condition of toxemia. As a rule the intelligence is not impaired in these cases, but the faculties of attention and association are impaired and that gives the impression of feeble mindedness. Another was a girl deaf and dumb, and it is easy to see how this would handicap the examiners in trying to establish the mental status by questions the suspect is unable to understand. At Bellevue we use the performance tests by which the language difficulty is overcome. It is much like puzzles and certain acts test the memory and judgment. This girl did these very well. Although she had only been in this country a year she understood and could read English sufficiently so that it was not necessary to give her instructions in pantomine, which certainly showed that she was not feeble minded; nevertheless, she was being considered for deportation on this ground.

Another matter for thought is just where we draw the line in barring out an immigrant, what de we require when we demand the qualities that will make for citizenship. Many of the so called radicals are not feeble minded, and high grade morons might fit into our social scheme beautifully for they are faithful workers, will do work that others will not do, and are not so apt to be discontented, engage in strikes, etc., although it must be admitted they are very susceptible to suggestion and would follow where others led. It is my opinion, regarding group tests, that they would be only partially successful in this problem. To be sure, the group tests could be used in the selection of those undoubtedly above par, but for the others individual tests would have to be used to judge their real mental status because of their emotional condition. The I. Q. varies from 10 to 20 points according to the emotional state of the individual examined. Another practical concideration is whether we could educate the public to see the necessity of appropriating a sum sufficient to carry on this work that Dr. Lawrence proposes which would undoubtedly be valuable if we could make them see the practicability of it.

Dr. Smith Ely Jelliffe: The most promising thing, as I think over the various topics brought to our attention, is that there is so much interest in the situation,—that brains are being counted as worth something. You all know how difficult it was for a man with flat feet to get into the army, but a man with a flat brain had no difficulty at all. How are we going to keep the flat brains out? I pause somewhat when I recall what Dr. Lawrence said (I think these figures are his): that in 750,000 aspirants for the United States Army 50 per cent. were below the mental age of 12 years. It does not seem to me that the problem is, in view of this, so much how to keep out the feeble minded as it is what to do with those who are here. If our Secretary of State struck the right note in proposing a naval vacation, I think that vote to bring about a more stringent type of immigrant vacation might be taken so that we could catch up with these twelve year old people, and we could devote our efforts to educate those we have at home and not spend so much time in sifting out new arrivals.

I think that some of Dr. Lawrence's suggestions were rather pertinent. It seems to be the problem of the feeble minded is one of the largest civilizaton has to meet. Those of you who see me to-day mght never guess that I was once a slim sapling, but it was so, and at that time running was such a favorite sport of mine that I was in danger of indulging in it to the extent of running off my own feet. Civilization is running off its own feet. Undoubtedly the machine has outrun the intelligence necessary to direct it. Though we talk of intelligence, we have not enough intelligence to run the machine and it is racing now to collapse. So one bite at the cherry would not be sufficient to eliminate some of the factors.

Certain features interested me in the way of practical issues. Any of you who have crossed the ocean in recent years know with what difficulty one approaches the time of landing and how everything that could have been distributed. over the eight or nine days of the voyage has to be done in the last two or three hours. It is the same thing in passing through many immigrants in a few moments on landing here; whereas, carefully distributed work on the other side and in the ports of exit where there are more adequate ways of handling the problem would prevent the necessity for this. It always seems that we are better able to bring up the difficulties and fallacies in discussing a problem than we are to offer constructive arguments.

Mr. J. L. Stenquist: We have a situation here with two aspects; first, is it desirable to take some action in this matter. It seems to me it is. The other phase is, how well can we do this sifting process. Working on this front—and I am somewhat interested in that,—there are a few general statements that can be made. First of all we think at first of the enormous number, and of the magnitude of the thing. The people of whom we are speaking amount to 10 per cent., so that out of every hundred we would have from five to ten people with whom we are seriously concerned. For that reason it seems to me practicable to set up a rapid working machine to sift all these people quickly and easily, and at comparatively small expense, and so differentiate the questionable cases and turn these over to the various professions, and there is no question but in this way we could do much more than we are doing now. Even if a few mistakes were made, the degree of progress would be so great that we could overlook the possibilities of mistakes. I would also urge the point made by Dr. Blanchard of the necessity for the highest talent, the highest training for these examiners. The one outstanding answer to that troublesome point is, of course, the present alternative; what do we do now We look at them for one minute and determine their mental status and the physician is asked to determine their physical status in the same number of seconds. Almost anything would be an improvement over that. The figures of Dr. Lawrence present a formidable array of evidence to show the tremendous importance of this type of thing.

Dr. Antonio Stella: I beg permission to take exception to some of the statements made bv Dr. Lawrence. I was shocked at some of his utterances regarding Italians. I am not speaking from a biased point of view, but there are some impressions he may have made that ought to be corrected. He practically made the Italian appear at the head of the list of criminals and defectives; he spoke of the Italians as being in the front line in the percentages of the vagrants and dependents. If I remember correctly from a report of the Department of Charities; there are fewer Italians in the poor house than any other nationality. On Wards Island they occupy the twelfth line. Regarding prostitutes, it has been the boast of our Police Commissioner that with an Italian population of 700,000 there are no Italian prostitutes, there is not a woman on the street in this city, except in Mulberry Street, where there are five or six listed as such in the most crowded Italian quarter of the city. When we think of the great temptation the young Italian girl, living in poverty, working in factories for long hours and small pay, is exposed to, this is a remarkable record. In regard to dependency, there never was an Italian found in the bread line that was supplied with food in the old days by Fleischman's bakery. If they are unemployed they take the first steamer home to Italy. They are really birds of passage and when work stops they fly away. They are doubly selected.

When an Italian decides to come to this country it takes moral and physical courage. They are examined at the port of embarkation by an American physician and re-examined at Ellis Island, and they are an extremely healthy lot of people. They are exposed to dangerous occupations so that many contract tuberculosis, but they go home to die. It is the same with syphilis; there is very little venereal disease among Italian immigrants, and this is shown by the fecundity of the Italian women. But they do acquire syphilis in this country. The delinquency of Italian children is the result of their living in the slums in the most congested sections of the city. Also, the public school system, wonderful as it is in many aspects, is responsible for the loss of authority in the parents. They learn things at school of which their parents are ignorant and come to regard them as inferior and altogether flout their efforts to train them as the parents themselves were trained in habits and thoughts of decent living. That is what makes them criminals, and it is the second generation, the children born and brought up in this country, who constitute the criminal element among the Italians. Regarding the intelligence of the Italians, I was surprised to hear that they have been listed below the negroes. Dr. Maxwell always said that the school reports showed the Italian children the most promising of any race. It would be possible for a race with such a history of greatness to so degenerate as to breed children not proficient in the public schools.

We ought really to be most grateful to Dr. Blanchard for her observations on the fact that the emotions bring about a condition in Italians which makes them appear stupid. I have seen some who had been classified as feeble minded who had at the time of examination been undergoing great emotional crises. My attention was recently directed to the case of a woman wo had raised a family of seven children and brought them to this strange country; she refused food when one of her children has been separated from her and sent to a hospital for traucoma. This woman was suspected of mental instability and was questioned, the questions containing the form the suspicion took. She was asked, "Are you afraid to eat because you believe the food is poisoned?" She replied, "Madonna mia, I cannot eat," and repeated "Madonna mia!" a number of times. Then they asked her did she hear voices, did she believe she was talking with God, and her reply, in my

33

opinion, expressed more sense than they exhibited; she answered that she regarded herself unworthy to talk with God.

I believe the United State has the right to keep away all immigrants, but when it comes to applying these tests in the most unschematic way without consideration for temporary psychotic states, I feel that great injustice is often done. I believe these examinations should be conducted at the port of embarkation in a systematic way and all this misery and tragedy could then be avoided. Over there, divided among many ports, they would have months, if necessary, for observation, and in that way the problem here would be eliminated. I think Dr. Lawrence would give an impression more consistent with the real facts, and one much more fair to the Italian race if the percentages were given with the population to give the ratio with which the percentage is arrived at.

Dr. G. Alfred Lawrence: Intelligence, of course, renders one able to make good use of education in successfully adjusting to the environment. In answer to Dr. Stella, I hasten to state that I had no wish to make any invidious comparisons between the people of different nationalities; the statistics I gave have been very carefully compiled and they are presented, not as representing my personal opinions, but as evidence of facts carefully gathered together by trained investigators. We want Italians in this country, bright and intelligent men, women and children, the best that Italy can send us; but we do not want those who make up the no inconsiderable percentage of criminals, and there are many of them in this country at this time. This is no reflection on the Italian people; it is merely a statement of facts as they exist in this country at present.

In regard to Dr. Blanchard's suggestion, illustrated by the cases of the two women, one in a post syphilitic condition and the other deaf and dumb, I do not think any injustice would have been done had they been excluded. It would be difficult to make some of these tests. Look at those three or four families I quoted; the Jukes cost New York one million dollars in thirty years, and another alien half a million. We have enuogh morons in this country already to do all the work they are capable of doing, and we do not need any more. We should exclude any element that cannot be of economic and productive value in this country. Probably 50 per cent. of the citizens of the United States are of the mental status of 12 years or under, so we have enough subnormality in the country. We are now admitting only 3 per cent. of any nation according to the percentage of the population here of that country; why not have this 3 per cent. of the best instead of the worst? We can do that by these intelligent tests. We can use general group tests and use such tests as a sieve to detect the markedly defective, and by intensive study of these, few cases of injustice will occur. Many insane and many markedly defective get in at the present time. Some cases certified for deportation have been examined and re-examined, resulting each time in the statement being made that they were defective, and yet orders have come from Washington that they be retained in this country. This, of course, is due to political pull, and cases of that kind should be proven, and this can only be done by arousing public sentiment. As far as immigrant defectives are concerned we should adopt the slogan, "They shall not pass."

CPSIA information can be obtained
at www.ICGtesting.com
Printed in the USA
BVHW09*1112160818
524721BV00018B/2452/P